I0151367

Don't Let The Feathers Fool Ya!

Cindy Barnes

DON'T LET THE FEATHERS FOOL YA!

ISBN: 0999294601

ISBN-13: 978-0-9992946-0-4

Table of Contents

DON'T LET THE FEATHERS FOOL YA!

DEDICATION

To everyone who is about to see yourselves from a *coop*, a *lake*, a *cliff*, a *branch*, a *ranch*, a *nest* or even an *iceberg*, get ready to laugh your way to victory as I humbly and with love dedicate this, my first book to my amazing parents who were always so proud of me, loved hearing about the newest great news I had to share and after an extra special sermon would walk up to the pulpit and whisper in my ear.... **"*Now that was another Top Ten!*"** May they enjoy Heaven after 60 years married and still holding hands! They showed their family & loved ones what it "Looked Like" to be Victorious & joy-filled in Christ. They left their footprints in the sand, leaving a lasting imprint and legacy for their loved ones to follow and I miss them every single day!

To my beloved James, my husband of 40+ amazing years who I met on a blind date thanks to my dad who knew we would be a perfect match! We fell in love, married, raised a beautiful family and enjoy sharing life together! In the midst of sharing our lives we found Jesus and that's when abundant life began! We shared the pulpit for 18 abundant years and on any given Sunday when I had the honor of bringing God's Word, you would find him sitting in the front row cheering me on! He has always been and continues to be my Prayer Support and Covering, my #1 Fan, my Protector, my Provider, my Best Friend, my Pastor, my Proverbs 31 Perfect Husband, the Father of the Year Every Year, my Forever Sweetheart and the Wind Beneath My

Wings - No Pun Intended!

To my children, grandchildren and *greaties* ... thank you for making life fun! I cannot imagine my world without every single one of you in it. I am Super Blessed. My *greatest joy* calls me Mom and my *sweetest gifts* call me Nana.

To my Sister Veralyn and Brother in Law Tim; thank you so much for not giving up on me, for praying for me and believing there would be a day that I would fall to my knees and ultimately receive Jesus Christ into my heart as my Personal Lord and Savior! I am certain it was the two of you that *"prayed me in"* .... I wouldn't be Heaven Bound if it wasn't for your incredible diligence to walk by faith and not by sight. God Divinely used you to bring into my life and heart my beautiful daughter, *'My Greatest Joy.'* (Psalm 113:9 - He gives the childless woman a family, making her a *happy mother.* Praise the Lord!)

You taught me how to be a great mother and a Godly wife, how to be a helper to my husband and answer the call of God which gave "US" the Faith and Joy that Pastoring and Preaching the Gospel for the past 22 years would bring! **Yes, TAKE A BOW, you deserve it!**

To my beloved brothers, Billy and Burke, I miss you every single day! I'm glad you are safe in our Father's Arms! I'll never understand why we had to say goodbye so soon but I am certain we will be together again in Paradise one day! I am honored to have been your little sister! (Yes, even my little brother Billy called himself my *Big Brother* and I loved that!) I always have and always will look up to you both! Rest in Peace and enjoy Heaven my sweet brothers!

To my extended family and friends as well as my Church family (First Lighthouse Community Church where my hubby and I served as Senior Pastors for 18 beautiful years and now The GLORY Chain where I have the honor of pastoring people from all over the world) thank you for sharing life with me, for making our church services so exciting and for always bringing love and encouragement into my world! I wish I could name *every single one of you* but I know that you know who you are and how much you each mean to me! **A special hug to Elena, Allie and Kath!**

TO MY LORD AND SAVIOR JESUS CHRIST
IT REALLY IS ALL ABOUT YOU!
You Rescued Me, Redeemed Me, Called Me, Anointed Me, Equipped Me, Inspire Me, Strengthen Me, Appointed and Gifted Me to Inspire Others Through Living the Truth, Preaching the Truth, Writing and Singing the Truth and Shining Bright the Truth ... ONE OF THE SONGS YOU WROTE THRU ME SAYS IT BEST:

MAY ALL I DO SOMEHOW POINT TO YOU
MY JESUS, MY REWARD!

Finally, to *all* who will read this, my first published book, I do hope and pray that you will find Jesus through the words of whimsy humor and light-heartedness. His sense of humor far surpasses most of ours and I pray He will use this book as a *tool* to help build up the Body of Christ and help you reach your *full potential* so that you might leave a legacy that others can follow. We've heard said that not everything that glistens is *GOLD* but if you'll prayerfully search for the many valuable *nuggets* buried within the pages paragraphs and chapters of this book the Holy Spirit will cause them to *SHINE* - pick them up, put them in your pocket and incorporate them into your everyday life.

Now the fun part! Whether you are beginning this journey from a *coop*, a *lake*, a *cliff*, a *branch*, a *ranch*, a *nest* or even an *iceberg*, put your shoulders back, hold your head up high, prepare to *SOAR* as you catch the next Holy Ghost air current and boldly say, as I have said and continue to say:

DON'T LET THE FEATHERS FOOL YA!
enjoy the FLIGHT!

INTRODUCTION

In this 19 Part short study *"Don't Let the Feathers FOOL YA"* we will discover that what we focus on most we will eventually become. What we spend our time doing we will eventually be defined as... and although this is simply not fair, the majority of the world absolutely does judge a book by its cover!

Every seed planted has the potential to take root, grow up, grow wings and become the cover of your book.

Some birds reflect God's gifts and callings while other birds reflect the way you and I can tend to *miss the mark* of God's perfect standard. Let not your heart be troubled ... help is on the way! In almost no time at all you can go *from being* overwhelmed by life *to being* over-comers of life!

"Don't Let the Feathers Fool Ya" will encourage you to **rise up** on wings of eagles, to **rise up** with faith

that moves mountains, to **rise up** with joy for the journey, to **rise up** with a song in your heart and to **rise up** with incredible love for a lost and dying world ... All of this while standing on the threshold of glorious praise and victory in Jesus!

My Hope is that you'll discover and/or rediscover the great difference between being *filled* with the Spirit and His Gifts 'versus' being *led* by the Spirit of these Gifts.

My Prayer is that your journey shall cause you to trust in and rely on the *Giver of Every Gift!*

God's Word is the Standard.   Following God's Word will always lead you to the Truth, and knowing the Truth will always set you free!

Think of yourself as a little birdie in a cage and the Lord walks over and *opens the door* .... He says "Be Free little birdie Be Free ... You are my Prized Possession. I paid the way to unlock your door .... now spread your little *wings* and fly .... and then Soar .... Soar on wings of Big Eagles little birdie and *never ever* look back!"

James 1:17-18 NLT
[17] Whatever is good and perfect is a gift coming down to us from God our Father, who created all the lights in the heavens. He never changes or casts a shifting shadow. [18] He chose to give birth to us by giving us His true Word. And we, out of all creation, became his prized possession.

CHAPTER #1
THE "WHO-T" OWL

This is the "*HOO-WHO*" in the Body of Christ! They are full of <u>wisdom's curiosity</u>, very inquisitive and eager learners. If not careful this Christian can become an '*Intrusive Busy Body*'... always looking for and gathering information to share with others. Exciting news usually turns into that "G" Word nobody likes to admit being a part of ... GOSSIP!

Definition of gossip - casual or unconstrained conversation or reports about other people, typically involving details which are not confirmed as true.

It might sound something like this:

"You'll never guess HOO-**WHO** I saw with **WHO** and you'll never believe it when I tell you **WHO** they were talking about!"

The "WHO-WHO" wants to share with the "YOU-YOU" anything you'll stand still long enough to hear! Gossip isn't only defined by the one spreading a particular rumor but there needs to be a listener or a set of "itchy ears" agreeing to sit quietly and take in all of the information.

Do your best to make sure it isn't you!

The way to stop the Owl from spreading gossip is to *"Nip It in The Bud"* ... You must rise up with Holy Ghost Boldness and say STOP to the gossiper! This will shake them up the first time because most of us will sit and listen then later wish we hadn't! Lovingly let them know that unless the news they are sharing is something to rejoice about or something that is their own good news to share then you will not be the 2nd guilty party of this gossiping duo .... The one speaking as well as the one listening are both guilty and will answer to the Lord one day for what was done in secret or behind the backs of others. Once you have taken a stand for righteousness the "Who-T" Owl will no longer try to whisper in your ear the secrets that are not his/hers to share.

The good news is that because of the Owls eagerness to learn, their keen eye for curiosity and their God-Given wisdom, with some Biblical teaching and patience the Owl in the body of Christ can go *from* a busy-body know it all *To* a man or woman of integrity, wisdom and counsel...

The Born Again and Transformed Owl always has *The Good Book* in his hands and would make a great Counsellor in the Body of Christ as the Lord puts His Super on their Natural God-Given Wisdom!

The Born Again and Transformed Owl would also make a great Teacher in the Body of Christ - Sunday school or part of the fivefold ministry teaching gift because of their God-Given gift of *wisdom's curiosity* as well as their inquisitive eagerness to learn, gather information and share with others! Where there's an Owl there is a BOOK! *The Holy Book*! The Good Book!

FUN FACT ABOUT OWLS:

Owls naturally have a keen sense of hearing and have great eyesight even in complete darkness!

A redeemed Owl in the body of Christ is keenly aware of what the Spirit is saying. the Bible says he who has ears let him hear what the Spirit is saying to the Church! The darkness of the enemy warfare does not cause the Owl to budge! He can see right through the lies of darkness and bring to *The Light* the strategies for us to follow according to God's Holy Word!

If you know somebody who portrays some of the UN-redeemed characteristics of the Owl, get the mighty intercessors praying for them to see Jesus reaching out to them because the owls are *extremely valuable* to the **"Marching Forward"** of the Body of Christ!

We need to **GIVE A HOOT** about our upcoming mighty Christian soldiers!

Meditate on:

Proverbs 4:6-7 TLB
[6] Cling to wisdom—she will protect you. Love her— she will guard you. [7] Getting wisdom is the most important thing you can do! And with your wisdom, develop common sense and good judgment.

Proverbs 17:4 ESV
An evildoer listens to wicked lips, and a liar gives ear to a mischievous tongue.

Matthew 12:36 ESV
I tell you, on the day of judgment people will give account for every careless word they speak.

Luke 6:31 ESV
And as you wish that others would do to you, do so to them.

CHAPTER #2
THE PARROT

This is the one who *REPEATS everything they hear!* They are usually very colorful and fun to be around. The Parrot's BFF is our friend **The Owl** which if not careful can be a *"Dangerous Duo"* ... imagine this conversation:

OWL: "Hey Parrot, HOOHOO my buddy my friend, I bet you'll never guess *'who'* I saw with *'who'*? I was just minding my own business and BOOM! There they were right before my eyes! I acted like I didn't see a thing! (HA)

PARROT: "Tell Me Everything!!!"

OWL: "Now make a 'Parrot Promise' that you won't tell anybody *who* told you *who* I saw with *who* because if you do 'You Know HOO' is gonna be mad!"

PARROT: "Won't tell anybody *who* was with *who* ... Won't tell anybody *who* was with *who* ... *who* was with *who* was with *who* ...

The Parrot quietly listens to all the owl has to say and then as soon as the first listening ear walks by He/She *repeats everything* shared in secret... Word for Word!!!

The Parrot is not a wallflower. The Lord made this Bird Colorful and Striking in the Body of Christ, and they love to be out in the front sitting on their perch talking to everybody who walks by! They are a people parrot or people person!

Left on their own they will repeat everything they hear. They won't think about whether or not it is right or wrong or whether it is appropriate or inappropriate. This is extremely dangerous in itself as it will tend to cause strife, wedges, arguments and disastrous conversations....

But Surrendered to Christ the Parrot makes a great leader in the church as they *repeat* what Jesus taught *word for word.* Many powerful Evangelists and Pastors are born again, Spirit led and surrendered to Christ parrots!

The Perch has been replaced with The Pulpit and the Gossip has been replaced with The Gospel!

FUN FACT ABOUT PARROTS:

Parrots are one of the most intelligent of all the bird species!

Meditate on:

Proverbs 18:21 ESV
Death and life are in the power of the tongue, and those who love it will eat its fruits.

Exodus 20:16 ESV
"You shall not bear false witness against your neighbor.

Psalm 19:14 ESV
Let the words of my mouth and the meditation of my heart be acceptable in your sight, O Lord, my rock and my redeemer.

Acts 4:31 NLT
After this prayer, the meeting place shook, and they were all filled with the Holy Spirit. Then they preached the word of God with boldness.

CINDY BARNES

CHAPTER #3
THE OSTRICH

This is the Christian who always seems to have *'lots of problems'* and rather than deal with them they just want them to ***POOF*** and Be Gone!

They would much rather run away and put their head in the sand ... put their head under the covers ... or shove everything under the carpet than to bother somebody to get the help or advice they desperately need.

Because the Ostrich is so large, their appearance alone gives the world the wrong impression that they are strong, aggressive and out-going .... but most Ostriches came from a family growing up that said things like:

"Children are to be *seen* and *not* heard!"

They might remember hearing things like:

"Don't bother us unless you are bleeding"

"Go outside and play, it's NOT dark yet"

"Go watch TV"

"Go do your homework"

"Go do something"

"Go do anything"

"Just GO!"

And the Ostrich learns through wrong teaching that unless you have a problem that is a matter of life and death you are not valued and should remain silent. After being born again and set free from the past, they still tend to struggle with their newfound victory. More times than not the ostrich continues to see themselves as little children being a bother.

The dilemma that follows is that they look strong on the outside but what's on the inside remains hidden. They walk around with a mask on acting as if all is well when it's really not and they don't know what to do about it.... *But God!*

Our God of Love Mercy and Victory continues ministering to their heart until finally the ostrich waves the white flag and completely surrenders, giving the Lord everything that they once thought was truth for the gift of receiving the God of *All Truth* so that once and for all they can see themselves through the eyes of Love and ultimately become all that God has called them to be!

Immediately after, you will hear the *grandest loudest boldest Ostrich Shout of Hallelujah*, when the miracle happens...

Jesus becomes the Father they always wanted! He becomes a true *Best Friend and Mentor*. As the Lord reaches out to them and lovingly convinces them that they can reach out to Him or call to Him anytime, anywhere for any reason, it's not long before God's mercy gift is revealed in a *big way*. They get set free to become everything that the Lord created them to be. A friend to the friendless, a mentor within the Body of Christ and one who quickly notices others who have walked a similar road. What happens next might cause *you* to shout Hallelujah....

As the Big ole ostrich who once was timid shy and so lost now portrays that mighty Christian warrior, shining super bright and filled with God's purpose to give away what was freely given, it is as if the Lord gives them 20/20 *Super Vision* to see those who the enemy wants to keep bound. The once shy Ostrich now struts right over to those the Lord leads them to and after an introduction and a big ole Ostrich hug simply takes them under his/her wing, gently removes their mask and says: "Have I got a story for you ....Oh and by the way, there's someone I'd like you to meet."

In the distance from every land near and far you'll from time to time hear a *grand, loud, bold shout* of *Hallelujah* and you'll know it's another Ostrich paying it forward!

To God be ALL the Glory!

Large and *'in charge'* the Ostrich begins most conversations with compassion and offers others the *Gift* of being a *Safe Friend* who will encourage those who have been hiding in their pain to trust God to give them a bright future and a secure hope!

FUN FACT ABOUT THE OSTRICH:

The Ostrich has the LARGEST Eyes of any land animal, almost 5cm across. This allows them to see the enemy coming from long distances away!

Meditate on:

Psalm 121:1 NIV
I lift up my eyes to the mountain, where does my help come from? My help comes from the Lord, the Maker of heaven and earth.

Jeremiah 29:11 NET
11 For I know what I have planned for you,' says the Lord.' I have plans to prosper you, not to harm you. I have plans to give you a future filled with hope.

CHAPTER #4
LARK SPARROW

This is our EARLY to RISE Christian! They begin their day getting *fueled up and praised up*! They are basically a cheerful type, mostly content... they know who they are in Christ and do not feel the need to prove it by what they say .... but instead they live it by *what they do*!

They tend to blend in with their surroundings, but once darkness begins to creep in you won't find the Lark Sparrow blending in any longer, in fact once it is the darkest hour you will hear the *War Cry Song* of radical praise and every demon will flee and all within earshot of this Intercessors Song will be FREE!

Personal Story: One beautiful Springtime morning my husband and I rescued a baby bird that was a brand new hatchling. It had fallen from a nest that was so high up in a tree that we were shocked it didn't die when it hit the ground.

Before we could pick it up, our trusty Labrador retriever named Buddy grabbed it! We said, "Drop It Buddy" .... He dropped It alright, but picked it up again before we could rescue it! In a panic we screamed "Drop It Buddy" and he dropped it but once again before we could rescue it, back in his mouth it went! The 3rd time we yelled our Loudest *"Drop It Drop It Drop It Buddy!"* and he reluctantly dropped the treasure! Little did he know what a treasure she would be!

That's when we met Hannah. She was just a little tiny gooey thing lying in the dirt. We picked her up and took her in the house and realized she was still alive! Praise God! We proceeded to wash her off, said some prayers over her and decided to try to hand feed this little blob with a beak. If you've never hand-fed A newborn bird let me tell you it is a full-time commitment! You must feed them every 15 to 20 minutes all day long! Imagine the mommy bird leaving the nest to get her children's meal and as she flies back to the nest all the babies begin to cry and chirp chirp chirp as she feeds them. By time the last one is fed the first one is almost ready for another bite (smile) so there she goes for more food.

The GOOD NEWS to raising baby birds is that they sleep all through the night. You may wonder why? Since their mommies cannot hunt at night because of the darkness the Good Lord in His mercy and grace gives them sweet dreams right after the sun goes down and all through the night. The minute the sun begins to rise up over the mountains you'll hear *chirp-chirp ... chirp-chirp ... chirp-chirp ...* and the first thing you'll do is rejoice that the baby lived through the night. The next thing you'll realize is that your busy day has begun!

Once Hannah got all of her feathers we thought she was a basic little sparrow but we were captivated by the beautiful black lines on her forehead so we looked it up in our bird book and found that she was in the sparrow family but actually defined as a Lark Sparrow. This would later become an important part of this story and a testimony of how God's creation teaches us spiritual nuggets that we can incorporate into our lives if we simply pay attention.

One night after Hannah realized she was not a baby any more we were sleeping and were woken up to what sounded like a *canary in the kitchen!* My husband and I got up and dashed to the kitchen only to find Hannah looking back at us as if to say "Hi Dad and Mom, what are you guys doing up?" We kind of shrugged our shoulders, looked at each other, shrugged our shoulders again, turned the lights off, went back to bed and would you believe it? The songs began again!

Come to find out the Lark Sparrow sings the song of the canary. It is the most beautiful *War-Cry Song* you'll ever hear and it doesn't begin until the darkest Hour! Every night at the midnight hour she would 'sing at the top of her lungs' and fill our home with *glorious praise!* Hannah was a joy and blessing to us. We often talk about that first day of her life and what a miracle it was that she lived through such a tragic beginning.

We considered Hannah to be a gift from God and our beautiful little blessing. She taught us that we too could sing a song of praise and prayer in the *darkest hours of our lives!*

She taught us by example how to wake up every morning being joyful thankful and content!

One afternoon I noticed Hannah leaning on the inside of the cage, heavy breathing, eyes closed, dying right before my eyes! She was eleven years old by now and I thought about all of the joy she had brought us and the life lessons she had taught me and I was not going to allow this **'dark hour'** to have her if my God would be merciful and save her *One More Time!* ..... I stood In front of that cage and I shouted out my own war-cry song!

I said: "Hannah, Be Healed In Jesus Mighty Name"

.... No change!

"Hannah, in the Name above every Name I say Be Healed! I Bind the spirit of death and I loose life in Jesus Name!"

... nothing

Dear Heavenly Father, please grant Hannah one more miracle! Breathe life back into her little body I pray!

.... what??????

She shook her head, shook her head again, looked up at me as if to say *"Thanks Mommy!"*

She was healed! God had granted her yet another miracle! This time I considered it a gift to me! She taught me how to pray the war-cry song in the midnight hour! Her example gave me the recipe to follow on that amazing day so long ago!

Our Hannah lived another 2 years after that miracle day! She spent most of *our waking hours* riding around on my shoulder and every night without fail we'd wake up at the stroke of midnight to Hannah singing war-cry songs of victory! She was 4 ounces of feathered beauty and she blessed our lives for 13 beautiful years.

In conclusion to the Lark Sparrows main qualities you may not notice the Lark Sparrow at first glance as they blend in with their surroundings. But they truly are a surprise gift in the Body of Christ when at the darkest hour in someone's life this Intercessor Prayer Warrior will Rise Up and pray with authority and power until the person being swallowed up by darkness is completely Set Free!

Do you know a Lark Sparrow? Maybe you are a Lark Sparrow? Whether it's you or someone you know, it is a given that you are an Intercessor and are being called to Intercessory Prayer.

You are an Intercessors "war-cry" Prayer Warrior!

Your war cry may not sound like a canary, but it will be a "Tongue" that will drive every demon away in the mighty Name of Jesus!

Your ministry will be best served on the Prayer Team and you have the ability the lead the way.

You would make a great Intercessory Prayer Team Leader.

Meditate on:

2 Thessalonians 1:11-12 NLT

[11] So we keep on praying for you, asking our God to enable you to live a life worthy of his call. May he give you the power to accomplish all the good things your faith prompts you to do. [12] Then the name of our Lord Jesus will be honored because of the way you live, and you will be honored along with him. This is all made possible because of the grace of our God and Lord, Jesus Christ.

Chapter #5
THE CANARY

This is the Worshipper in the Body of Christ! They rise up early with a song in their heart and will sing all day long. Unlike the Lark Sparrow, the bright color of the canary tells us that they do not blend in and actually love to be center stage in front and noticed by everybody! They love leading people in song.

Put a tambourine in their hand and they will make music with it! Put a microphone in their hand and they will usher in God's Holy Presence with their gift of Worship and Praise!

This is our **'Worship Team'** consisting of our *Worship Leader* our *Song Leader* our *Director of Music* or our *Choir Director* in the Body of Christ. They simply need to be doing music somewhere. If there is no opening for Director or Leader they will be the shining star on any worship team! They have the gift of worship and song and are contagious in their love for Jesus as they come into His presence with thanksgiving in their hearts and give Him glorious praise!

This gift also embraces the Warrior Musicians in the body of Christ! Each one on the team worshipping together but in one accord. The singers of melody and harmony, the music from the drummer, the keyboard player, the violin or fiddle, the bass and electric guitar, the bongos and congas, the tambourine, the dancers ... The TEAM!

It only takes one heart filled with worship to bring an entire congregation into the throne room of God's Holy Grace so whether your church has a lone man or woman pluckin' a guitar and singing or a worship team or even an entire church choir, as the worship goes up the Presence Comes Down!

Do you see yourself in the canary? If you do it would be wise to join the choir, interview for the worship team, let your Pastor know that you are being called to the music ministry. Believe me, once you find your God Given Gift you will never feel empty again! Take it from me who led worship for a long time. As the Holy Spirit would fall upon us in response to our praise and love to Him I would stand in awestruck wonder as His Presence filled the place and I'd wonder how I could be so lucky to do the thing that I could not, not do??

Can you imagine when we get to Heaven and receive our rewards for doing something that we could not _NOT_ do?

We serve an awesome God!

FUN FACTS ABOUT CANARIES:

Canaries are not picky when it comes to eating, in fact canaries actually like **Jalapeno Peppers!** These peppers are rich in vitamins A and C. Jalapeno peppers also promote a healthy blood circulation and keeps the weight of your pet bird in check.

But of course, in order to keep your pet canary healthy, <u>a good quality seed mixture is a perfect diet</u> for them. You could also offer them greens such as spinach, collard greens, broccoli, cucumbers, squash, etc. They also eat oranges, bananas, apples, corn and strawberries.

Meditate on:

<u>Psalm 71:8</u> NIV
8 My mouth is filled with your praise, declaring your splendor all day long.

CINDY BARNES

Chapter #6
THE PENGUIN

This is our Christian that is **set in their ways.**
They were taught a certain way and will believe this
'one way' for the rest of their lives. This is the Old-
Time Religion Deacon type, some might call it the
Religious Spirit or one bound by the Law. In other
words, everywhere they look it's *BLACK & WHITE!*
They tend to become puffed up and arrogant but it
is simply because they are fighting for what they
truly believe.

Sadly, one who has the Penguin tendencies will
never actually take flight.

You might see them pacing back and forth and hear
them saying things like: *'we've done it this way for
45 years and I don't see any reason to change it
now'*

All in Favor? and everyone who wears the same black & white suit says Aye!

With patience, lots of love and great leadership the Penguins will be encouraged to gather under the waterfall of God's continual flow of love and blessings. Eventually the Spirit of God will begin to soften their hearts and *some* shall even respond by surrendering to the Holy Spirit and find that being black and white doesn't mean that they cannot live their lives in *Full Color!*

It is just thrilling to get to know a Penguin that has been set free from narrow mindedness and now lives in complete surrender and freedom as they are literally baptized and filled with the Holy Spirit and the mind of Christ. One who once lived within the Grey Area of Black & White now lives in Full Color as an amazing servant of the Lord that will happily look for ways to be a blessing by helping others in servant ministry!

SERVANT MINISTRY with others who are like-minded is the *new and improved* focus of the Penguin. They shine the brightest when they know they are filling a need. They also make a great Deacon or Elder and can be trusted with finances and important business dealings of the church. One who was once set in their ways are now extremely dependable and trustworthy to accomplish whatever is set before them, and they will do it with purpose and will remain in step with the program!

One may never actually see a Penguin fly but I have heard about those Penguins whom the Son has set Free running on the Ice and yelling:
"WEEEEEEE!"

NOTE:

Arrogance tears down and *Demolishes*
doing everything their way

Love *Builds Up* and is Constructive!
doing everything God's way

Meditate on:

Romans 7:6 NLT
But now we have been released from the law, for we died to it and are no longer captive to its power. Now we can serve God, not in the old way of obeying the letter of the law, but in the *new way* of living in the Spirit.

FUN FACT ABOUT PENGUINS:

As mentioned above Penguins are extremely Faithful. Most species of penguins keep the same partner for their entire life!

Chapter #7
LOVE BIRDS

These are our **Mercy Gifts** in the Body of Christ! They are the warm hug, the extra shoulder if you need one and the friend that will do their best to understand, especially when others don't!

Are you often drawn to people who are suffering or in distress?

Does helping the sick, needy, disabled, elderly, etc. excite you?

Do you find yourself wanting to participate in ministries that work with job placement, food pantries, shelters, assisted living homes?

IF THE ANSWER IS YES, YOU ARE A LOVEBIRD!

The Love Birds make great Encouragers, Greeters and Prayer Team Members in the Body of Christ. Everyone will flock around the 'Love Bird Ministry'! They work well with others understanding the gift of being in One Accord! They show the rest of the church what it 'looks like' to stand together to be stronger! Most nurses are lovebirds! You'll know them by their fruit of love and kindness. They have the gift of comforting you when you are in distress.

Everyone loves the Love Bird because they will sit and listen to our woes all day long BUT it is very important that within the group is someone who will help encourage and warn the love birds not to allow this to happen. Once you have given that warm hug, that extra shoulder and that sweet friendship then it is time to send your friend to someone with the Teaching Gift.

This will be a three-fold blessing:

1. It will help your friend to not get stuck in the quicksand of Warm Hugs...

2. It will help keep you, the Love Bird from taking on the Weight of the World and becoming Overweight yourself!

3. It will free you up for your *next assignment.*

Once you've prayed and ministered to someone, 'Let it GO' - *Give their burdens to God right along with them* and then send them on to the next ministry partner that will help them to Grow Up or what I like to say help them chew swallow & "GULP."

It's one thing to be loved and encouraged, but if we do not eat chew swallow and grow then the Love Birds will have a full-time ministry of stunting the growth in the Body of Christ. So send them ON to the Teaching Gift and the Lord will bring you another assignment.

Isn't it fun to begin to 'see' how we must work together in the family to fulfill God's call for us to be *One Body*?

Meditate on:

Romans 12:15-18 NAS
15 Rejoice with those who rejoice, and weep with those who weep. 16 Be of the same mind toward one another; do not be haughty in mind, but associate with the lowly. Do not be wise in your own estimation. 17 Never pay back evil for evil to anyone. Respect what is right in the sight of all men. 18 If possible, so far as it depends on you, be at peace with all men.

FUN FACTS ABOUT LOVEBIRDS:

Lovebirds have high levels of oxytocin in their brains (also known as the *love hormone*). This means that the bonds they create are deep and meaningful. Due to the intensity of the bond they develop with their mates they are one of the few animals on earth who mate for life.

CINDY BARNES

Chapter #8
THE ROOSTER

This is the Confident Christian! They love to lead, keep an eye out for predators, 'Rise Up Early' and of course think that everybody else should too! Because they are so confident they need to fight the urge to not come across as COCKY!

They love to be in charge of the Chickens and have the gift to become Great Leaders. They are very prophetic and you'll often hear them at the top of their lungs telling everyone to Get Up!! Rise UP!!! Don't Sleep your Day Away!!! But until they allow the Spirit of Grace, Patience and Love to fill their hearts, what most of us hear is: **COCK A DOODLE DOO!**

They prefer to work alone. They are confident to claim new territory. They don't necessarily work well with others of their own kind, but as long as the Rooster has a bunch of "groupies" he is happy! We will talk about that later in our chapter on the chickens.

Now, let's talk about the *Surrendered Rooster*. The Spirit Filled Rooster makes a Great Leader! Their Prophetic Anointing is powerful in the Body of Christ. As they grow in their calling they find that working together with other leaders will allow them to get so much more done. They learn that if they share the platform and the workload they will have a Power House Church filled with people who are excited and *sold out for Christ*!

The Spirit Filled Rooster makes a great Pastor. Their Prophetic and Apostolic Anointing creates a Ministry Leader that's not afraid to Claim 'new' Territory for the Lord and share their plan with *great enthusiasm and leadership*! The Holy Spirit helps them in their tendency to go from *'telling everyone what to do'* to becoming a great shepherd that will *'lead the team'* with confidence giving them someone they can look up too and follow. They are not known for their patience or mercy but they will build a team that will be balanced with all of the gifts so that the needs of their congregation will be met with strategic leadership, patience mercy and love. If the Rooster is married it would do him or her well to marry someone who has a similar call but someone with a softer edge along with the gift of nurture and mercy. You'll find this often in the Husband and Wife Pastoral Team.

Meditate on:

Titus 1:7-9 NLT

[7] A church leader is a manager of God's household, so he must live a blameless life. He must not be arrogant or quick-tempered; he must not be a heavy drinker, violent, or dishonest with money. [8] Rather, he must enjoy having guests in his home, and he must love what is good. He must live wisely and be just. He must live a devout and disciplined life. [9] He must have a strong belief in the trustworthy message he was taught; then he will be able to encourage others with wholesome teachings and show those who oppose it where they are wrong.

FUN FACTS ABOUT ROOSTERS:

Roosters are mostly aggressive as compared to the females. It is his responsibility to look after his hens and chicks and take care of their safety and also to see they are able to eat without being disturbed by other roosters. They are *Born To Be LEADERS*!

CINDY BARNES

Chapter #9
THE ROADRUNNER

This is our *'Nibbler'* in the Body of Christ. The Christian that *runs* from one meeting to another. I *need a Word!* I *wanna Word!* I *Gotta get a Word! God I need a Word!*

This Christian has learned to get by on *very little* water. They are convinced that a little bite here and a little bite there is perfectly fine as they *Run Run Run* from one house of worship to another. You'll hear the Roadrunner say things like:

I just *'love'* the Preacher over here but I *'love'* the worship over there. Oh, and *I 'love'* the people at this other amazing place ... and I can't wait to drive to the city where this super lay back church feeds you lunch as you listen on the outdoor lawn! ... Wow it's just GREAT and hey, did you hear that *Sister*

Sally is speaking in Alabama and *Brother Bob* is speaking in California? I'm going to try to get to both of those meetings!

The Road Runner can get completely worn out **running everywhere and being planted nowhere**. Some of the issues that I've noticed with this type of Christian service is:

1. Where is your HOME Church?

I am concerned that if we do not plant ourselves somewhere that we call *'Home'* then when a situation in life arises when you may need your Pastor or the church family to reach out to you, whether it's for encouragement or something more serious they might never even realize that you are MIA (missing in action) because you are not a faithful member of the family. You may not think that this time will ever come but take my word for it after being in the ministry for 22 years, *the time will come* and it is so very important for the leaders of the church to know who their members are so that they can make sure that they are caring for you past the Sunday morning sermons. Being a faithful member is key!

Hebrews 10:24-25
24 And let us consider one another to provoke unto love and to good works: 25Not forsaking the assembling of ourselves together, as the manner of some is; but exhorting one another: and so much the more, as ye see the day approaching.

2. Where do you Tithe?

Giving of donations or offerings with a cheerful heart is Biblical but it is also Biblical to give a tenth or a tithe of your income to the storehouse (your church) so that there will be enough supply to maintain the functioning and running of that particular church and its vision.

Some churches are called to minister to their city- *citywide vision.*

Some churches are called to minister to their nation- *nationwide vision.*

Some churches are focused on their state- *statewide vision.*

Some are called to a *Global Vision.*

As you begin to look for a church that fits you it is important not to choose a church that is the closest, the coolest, the fanciest, the most layback or the one with all of your friends, but it is most important that the church you plant yourself in is a church with a similar vision that the Lord has put in your heart. Then it is up to us to help support that vision by giving of our time our talent and our tithes and offerings.

If you are attending different churches every week you will have no place to help support and although it may not be a sin to pick and choose I do not believe it is in the best interest of yourself or your family. It is hard enough to get the support we need to live for Christ as it is, and I believe having a church family to call your own that you help support will be a family that will embrace and help support you. It is the safest way to stay connected!

This is also the way that the general bills are paid. Sometimes we forget that the electric company, the phone company, the rent, ministry items, food and drinks, communion supplies, maintaining the gardens, paying your Pastors salary and other miscellaneous is still to be paid every month just like your electric bill, your car, your phone, your food, your garden, etc. I have actually heard Christians say "WOW I never ever thought about who pays to keep the lights on and the air conditioning going to keep us comfortable each Sunday much less a building for us to meet in (smile) .... *Food for Thought!*

Malachi 3:10 AMP

[10] Bring all the tithes (the tenth) into the storehouse, so that there may be food in My house, and test Me now in this, says the Lord of hosts, if I will not open for you the windows of heaven and pour out for you [so great] a blessing until there is no more room to receive it.

3. Where do you SERVE?

Where are you going to be planted long enough to serve? Just because the Roadrunner can live on very little water does not mean that it should! We need to be well watered in the Word every day and to keep a commitment like that it is best that we commit our lives somewhere! Find that *'home'* that fits you the most and then allow your roots to go down into the soil of God's Marvelous Love. Offer yourself as a member to the leadership and you will see in a very short time that you will not have that need to run from one place to another, but to simply *'run to win'* with the rest of the beautiful people who will become your Church Family!

Psalm 122:1

I was glad when they said to me, "Let us go into the house of the LORD."

As we read in Psalm 122:1, David loved it when it was time to worship God. We should have the same joy today.

Psalm 100:2

Serve the Lord with gladness; Come before His presence with singing.

The Roadrunner can now appreciate the miracle of having Red Shoes and the simple Faith to Believe! AAAAaahhhh!

Redeemed and no longer running, our Roadrunner is a great friend because they have learned the blessing of community and communion within the body of Christ. They know who their family is and their family know them. They have a similar vision for the *'heartbeat'* of their church and are glad to help support it with their time talent and treasure. They are excited to serve the Lord by serving others. They have found that even though they once lived on very little water, there is nothing more thirst quenching than standing at the altar to minister to the Lord with their hands in total surrender while the outpouring of the Holy Spirit ministers to them a continual downpour of God's Love & Waterfall Blessings!

They appreciate their new-found family and on any given day you just might notice the Roadrunners standing under the waterfall wearing their Red Shoes shouting: **"There's No Place Like Home!"**

Meditate on:

John 7:38 TLB
[38] For the Scriptures declare that rivers of living water shall flow from the inmost being of anyone who believes in me."

FUN FACTS ABOUT ROADRUNNERS:

Roadrunners are not afraid of snakes and in fact are called Snake Killers because their favorite dinner is Rattle Snake!

They can live on very little water getting most of what they need from the foods they eat. Reminds me of Us, as we eat from the Bread of Life or the Word of God it is also called the Living Water!

Chapter #10
THE DOVE

This is the PEACEMAKER in the Body of Christ! Making Peace, Doing Peace, Living Peacefully. The Spirit of God's Peace shines from them as they live and walk in Peace!

The Doves manifest the Symbol of Peace – the Symbol of Beauty – the Symbol of Innocence and Wisdom.

The Dove is also quiet tempered, soft spoken and filled with graceful mercy. They are gifted in helping people resolve their differences and come back to the place of peace. They walk in Love and are extremely faithful to the ones they love.

Matthew 10:16 (Jesus Speaking)
"I am sending you out like Sheep among the Wolves, therefore be as *shrewd as snakes* and *innocent as*

doves. <u>Shrewd means</u>: *'being wise in the ways of the enemy'* and <u>Innocent as Doves means</u>:
'Be above reproach, living lives that are pleasing to God and to do harm to nobody'.

This Christian is sensitive but powerful. They are also sensitive to hearing from the Lord to give a powerful word. The Dove is someone who is easy to be around. You instantly feel at home when you're around a Dove, therefore they are someone that can speak wisdom and truth into your life and do it with gentle kindness.

What is peace? We often define it in terms of what it isn't—as in, it's the absence of conflict or distraction or anything that makes us feel uncomfortable or disturbed. But the gift of Peace is being relaxed and comfortable even in the midst of a storm. Hallelujah!

Having the gift of Peace is also having the gift of Faith. They go *'hand in hand'*. Peace in the Storm is having Faith believing that God is overseeing, directing and conducting all that is around us or surrounding us and we can rest knowing all is well with our soul.

Peace comes from knowing that God is in control.

Isaiah 26:3
You will keep in perfect peace all who trust in You, all whose thoughts are fixed on You!

The Dove makes a great Christian Counsellor, Life Coach or Mentor within the body of Christ!

Meditate on:

<u>Proverbs 12:20</u>
Deceit is in the hearts of those who plot evil, but those who promote peace have joy.

<u>FUN FACTS ABOUT DOVES:</u>

Doves have been used as messengers for thousands of years, particularly during war times. The male and female doves mate for life and are extremely sweet companions to one another.

CINDY BARNES

Chapter #11
THE STORK

This is the Christian that *'wears a lot of Hats'*! Their plate is Always Full but Never Too Full! They have the *Gift of Organization* and they Love Birthing New Projects!

They Love the **LABOR PAINS** of starting up something new or giving 'Birth' to a New Ministry, New Idea, New Department, New baby!

This is our **GIFT OF ADMINISTRATION** in the body of Christ.

A *kubernesis* 'in the Greek' was a steersman for a ship. He had the responsibility of bringing a ship into the harbor—through the rocks and waves and under all types of pressures.

The Stork has the Gift of Leading, Ruling, Organizing, Governing, and Administering .... These are some of the various words that come from different translations of the Scriptures of the same Greek word ADMINISTRATOR.

These Church Leaders are the ones steering the Church in the direction the Wind of the Spirit leads them. Whether they are called to preach and/or teach or whether they are directing activities or in charge of the managing of the office, the Stork will lead their team with expertise and grace.

They can find their niche in many different ministries and getting them to choose one to be planted in is a challenge to most storks but the majority who know them or serve alongside them will tell you that wherever the Stork has landed the church is *so very thankful to have them.*

Many times people of other gifts are jealous of the stork who just seems to be successful at everything they do, but it is simply the gift of administration at its optimum level. Don't try to compete with the Stork, but shine bright where you hang your hat!

The prescription for the Stork is to understand that they are NOT Important because of all that they *can do*, but because of *all that Jesus is in and through them.*

Meditate on:

2 Corinthians 9:12 KJB

For the ministry of this service is not only fully supplying the needs of the saints, but is also overflowing through many thanksgivings to God.

FUN FACTS ABOUT STORKS:

The legend about storks bringing babies got started in Victorian times. When a child asked, *"Where did I come from?"* the parents simply said *"The stork brought you."* This tied in nicely with the fact that European white storks often built their nests on the roof and chimney of houses in the spring, a time when many babies are born. The bird became a symbol of fertility and is considered good luck.

CINDY BARNES

Chapter #12
THE TURKEY

This is the Christian I've Lovingly named the *'High Maintenance Friend,'* someone who seems to have a problem almost all the time. They start out respectful and so very thankful for the time that you can or will set aside for them. As they become more comfortable they also become less respectful as they begin to GOBBLE UP your Time – GOBBLE UP your Day – GOBBLE UP your Night – GOBBLE UP your Tomorrow and GOBBLE UP your Tomorrow Night too!

The problem with the Turkey isn't really a problem at all. This bird has practiced a wrong mindset allowing their wrong thoughts to become a pattern of wrong choices and wrong living. The end result is a wrong state of mind. The Turkey has allowed boredom and laziness to become extreme loneliness and instead of allowing the Lord to give them a full and fulfilling life serving others, they instead require a need to be loved (instead of needed) then unfortunately begin creating problems in their lives that will require something from others.

The MERCY Gifts who are the Doves and the Love Birds in the Body of Christ will FLOCK around the Turkey but eventually it becomes apparent that the Turkey doesn't really need advice or counseling, they simply need to spend a few days with the Rooster or the Stork and learn some new techniques and ways to be *Full and Fulfilled* in their walk with the Lord.

Their mind, now filled with proper thinking causes them to do a complete 180!

Oh then you've got a whole different situation ... You'll have A friend that celebrates their day by giving God thanks and praise all through the day! They go from being lonely needy and greedy to being filled needed and generous with THANKSGIVING and GIVING THANKS all the more as the Lord leads! They cannot wait to hear the Roosters morning song so they can start their day with..... yep, you got it ... PRAISE & THANKSGIVING!

A TURKEY that has been Set Free is a wonderful friend to have! If you have ever spent a day or two with someone who is constantly Giving Thanks to the Lord you will yourself be set free! FREEDOM is birthed thru **THANKSGIVING!**

A **<u>Set Free Turkey</u>** makes a Great Team Leader! A Great Greeter, Hospitality Team Member, Servant Ministry, Sunday School or Preschool Teacher and a great all round friend!

Meditate on:

Psalm 107:8-9 NIV
[8] Let them give thanks to the LORD for his unfailing love and his wonderful deeds for mankind, [9] for he satisfies the thirsty and fills the hungry with good things.

FUN FACT ABOUT THE TURKEY:

To debunk a popular turkey tale, Benjamin Franklin did not advocate for the turkey as the National Bird.

But he did call the Turkey a Bird of COURAGE!

CINDY BARNES

Chapter #13
THE VULTURE

The **VULTURE** has the ability to *Soar.* They were actually considered for the National Bird but when the eagle won out, the vulture chose to do everything he/she could do in their power to take from others what isn't theirs! They are known as "LAZY LEARNERS" and *Jealousy & Greed* is their sin.

They are Jealous of what you have.... Your Ministry – Your Anointing – Your Calling – Your Gifts and Graces –

Even though Your Ministry is not a *perfect fit* for the VULTURE, they don't care, they would rather take what doesn't fit and *'Try To Fit In'* just to say "Hey Look at What I found! - Look at Me!" ...

Just like a Vulture searches for **ROAD KILL** instead of searching for something fresh to eat, they want what's on **YOUR** Plate! They want **YOUR** Food but they don't want to earn the money to buy it. They want **YOUR** Education but they don't want to study to get it! They want **YOUR** Blessings, **YOUR** Calling, **YOUR** Gifts and **YOUR** Ministry!

Dealing with a Vulture takes lots of *Patience & Prayer*. They are greedy and do not see much wrong with it. Until the Lord becomes their King of Kings, Lord of Lords, Spirit of Power and Grace nothing much will change. But once the vulture truly lets the Spirit of Love have His way in and thru him/her and he/she truly becomes a New Creation, all Old Things Passed Away and they *Behold All Things Brand New*, a newly Redeemed Vulture will be excited about the new journey the Lord has in store. Once realizing that everything in front of them is Brand New the Vulture patiently waits for the Lord to reveal thru His Spirit what beautiful new paths he/she shall soar. An exciting truth is that God never said OOPS and this causes the Vulture's new outlook to be filled with Hope for a future filled with gladness no matter what gifted assignment the Lord has in store. It will be like waking up on Christmas morning every morning!

Meditate on:

2 Corinthians 5:17 (NKJV)
Therefore, if anyone *is* in Christ, *he* *is* a new creation; old things have passed away; behold, all things have become new.

FUN FACTS ABOUT VULTURES:

Vultures are High Flyers! Thermals help these birds to reach incredible heights, most of which would be deadly to other species of birds. Some species can live up to 50 years! A group of vultures is called a venue, and when circling the air, a group of vultures is called a kettle. Most vulture species mate for life.

CINDY BARNES

Chapter 14
THE CHICKEN

This is our SHY Christian, a bit of a Wallflower. They are afraid to try new things ... they tend to stick together with others of their kind ... likeminded .... *Fear of Failing* ... afraid of trying .... fearful of stepping out and taking a chance. They have the "But What if I Sink Syndrome" ... They want to get out of the boat but the fear of not being able to walk on water (or do the thing the Lord is asking) keeps them in the boat! They want to go to the other side but the fear of sinking keeps them many times from even getting in the boat! In other words they are flat out CHICKEN to try! The fear of failing has them paralyzed in their walk with the Lord so instead of moving forward they live a life of standing still and they do that scared to death! They have *'Stinkin' Thinkin'* which keeps them cooped up with other chickens of their kind. The Spirit of Fear and the lies from the pit of hell tells them that they never can soar, they never will soar, they'll always be less than their biggest dreams and the un-redeemed roosters continue to lie to their hens in the Chicken Coops all over the world and we must remember, the unredeemed Roosters along with the Chickens both have amazing gifts that are yet to be opened!

The chickens want to be RISK-TAKERS, they have such a longing to *Soar* like others they've met in the body of Christ, but until they look *Fear* right in the eyes and command the *'Spirit of Fear'* to loose their thoughts and minds and then receive and embrace the Gift of Faith they will never leave the *Stinkin-Thinkin Ground*!

All they hear all day long is: **Cluck Cluck I'm Outta Luck, if I was hockey I'd be a Puck, if I could swim I'd be a Duck but all I'll ever be is Stuck, Cluck Cluck I'm Outta Luck!**

They have been beaten down so badly from the one who rules the roost and from themselves allowing fear of failing and their stinkin' thinkin' to become their own negative chant that the more they pace back and forth and chant negativity nothing much will change for the future of the chicken..... but if they will stop and listen to the voice outside the coop things can change for them in just a moment or two!

The RECIPE for the chicken is this:

If you are AFRAID and the Lord asks you to step up and let your Faith in Him be your guide, then it is time to "*DO IT AFRAID!*" You will notice that as you take that Step in Faith the Darkness will *flee* and you'll be amazed as you step right OUT of the Chicken Coop and INTO your DREAM and High Calling! It is then that you'll be able to hear from the Lord and get excited about *Who you are in Christ* without a BIG Mouthed Rooster telling you what to do all day long!

Outside of the Chicken Coop are the REDEEMED and *Set Free Chickens* marching around the grounds holding up posters and signs with Philippians 4:13 ... no longer **CLUCKING** but **PROCLAIMING**: I Can Do All Things Through Christ Who Strengthens Me! As they continue their Prayer March, one by one chickens take the chance to **do it afraid** as they step out of the coop of fear and into complete freedom! As the Spirit of God falls fresh upon them the burden of fear no longer has them bound and after they shout HALLELUJAH in Chicken Talk, they join the march! Why? Although they are now free to go and do anything and everything they've always dreamed of doing *they can finally hear the Lords voice* and it is much LOUDER than the Roosters Demands as He gives them their assignment to show the ones filled with fear what it **LOOKS LIKE** to be Free!

To have been bound so long one would think they'd want to run as far away as possible but because they have love and mercy for the ones still lost there is nothing in their lives that will ever be more meaningful than to help others receive their gift of freedom!

Goodbye FEAR .... Hello FEAR NOT!

Meditate on:

Isaiah 41:10 TLB
Fear not, for I am with you. Do not be dismayed. I am your God. I will strengthen you; I will help you; I will uphold you with my victorious right hand.

Psalm 27:1 KJV
The LORD is my light and my salvation; whom shall I fear? the LORD is the strength of my life; of whom shall I be afraid?

2 Timothy 1:7 NKJV
For God has not given us the spirit of fear; but of power, and of love, and of a sound mind.

Psalm 56:3-4 KJV
When I am afraid, I will trust in thee.

FUN FACTS ABOUT CHICKENS:

Chickens have more bones in their necks than giraffes!

The fear of chickens is called Alektorophobia.

There are over 25 billion chickens in the world, that's more than any other bird –

May the Redeemed Chickens Continue Marching For Freedom & Victory over Fear!!

Chapter 15
THE DUCK

This is **THE QUACK** in the Body of Christ! Forgetting *'why'* they became what they became ... Like the ***rude doctor*** who used to dream about helping people, they lost their joy somewhere in the journey and are now known to many as **A Quack!!!** You'll also find this in the ***arrogant waitress*** or the ***cruel teacher*** in Elementary School? We've all met these people in our lives.

The truth is, they used to *'spin around dancing'* and DREAMING of becoming these things! The doctor just couldn't wait to ***'help people'*** .... The waitress couldn't wait to ***'serve people'*** and the teacher couldn't wait to ***'teach people'***, but eventually as time passed, they forgot to DAILY be Grateful for the Blessing of Helping, Serving and Teaching, and so they began to lose their passion and joy.

They literally *'forgot why they became what they became'*.... And now they hear their Patients, their Customers and their Students saying things like:

They are nothing but A QUACK!!! I want ANOTHER Doctor! I want ANOTHER Waitress! I want ANOTHER Teacher!

The sad truth is, these amazing people just need to remember why they became what and who they became! Get back on their knees and pray.... Ask Jesus to give them *His Passion Again* for Helping... *His Passion Again* for Serving.... *His Passion Again* for Teaching.... Then daily thank Him for the blessing.

And of course we all remember our Favorite Doctor who had a passion for helping us get better, and our Favorite Waiter or Waitress who always serves with a smile no matter what he/she might be going through at home, and of course our favorite teacher who encouraged us to be all we could possibly dream to be!

I'll always remember Dr. Kerchner who actually made house calls when I was so sick with spinal meningitis and ear infections. As scary as it was to have to go to the doctor so often I still remember his warm smile and tender voice. Then there was my 4th grade teacher Miss Roden who encouraged me to keep singing and in fact she also loved to sing and it was my favorite memory of 4th grade. And who could ever forget Mrs. Higgins, she was already a grandma when I first had her in 10th grade and she loved everything secretarial and is the teacher that taught me the skills that I still use today! I still brag to my sister that even though she was 3 years older and had won the 1st Place Top Speed "Gregg Award" for Typing and Shorthand, when I got there I beat her record! We both loved Mrs. Higgins and this is a fun memory we still talk about today!

These were DUCKS that not only pursued their high calling but embraced it with joy for the lifetime that they served! Continue doing the right thing because it is the right thing and the ones you'll minister to in your lifetime will remember you for their lifetime and God shall be glorified!

Meditate on:

Colossians 3:23-24 AMP
Whatever you do [whatever your task may be], work from the soul [that is, put in your very best effort], as if it is for the Lord and not for men, knowing [with all certainty] that it is from the Lord [not from men] that you will receive the inheritance which is your [greatest] reward. It is the Lord Christ whom you [actually] serve.

FUN FACTS ABOUT DUCKS:
Because a duck's eyes are located on either sides of its head, they have a field of vision of nearly 340 degrees. And thanks to the shape of their eyes, they can see objects both near and far simultaneously. To top it off, ducks can see in color.

CINDY BARNES

Chapter 16
THE PEACOCK

Question: After a fun shopping spree on a Saturday afternoon, who is more excited about Sunday Church .... You or your NEW OUTFIT?

This is the Christian who *Loves walking the Runway or strutting the Red Carpet*, who looks forward to coming to church to show everyone what they are wearing or to Show Off their New Outfit.

They are the DIVAS of the church who seem to find joy in comparing themselves to everyone around them and of course without really trying they somehow make others feel *'less than'* them in a very uncomfortable way.

They are All About the OUTWARD APPEARANCE! It is very hard for the Peacock to make friends due to the fact that they are always dressed to the *'nines'* ....

Others find it hard to compete with their colorful fancy wardrobe as well as their bright and colorful personality, and although the onlookers know they really shouldn't want to compete with the outward appearance of the peacock they have their own inward struggle of wanting to *'feel'* as beautiful as the Lord says they are.

Women find themselves *'secretly hating'* the peacock and men find themselves secretly taking an extra glance and they <u>both feel bad</u>.

and the enemy applauds!

The peacock lives to be noticed but until they allow the Lord to show them their True Beauty, their Inward Beauty, the Beauty of their Hearts, and their Identity in Christ, they will find themselves Showing Off, then hating themselves for doing it, only to plan for their next STRUT down the RUNWAY!

<u>The Recipe for the Peacock</u> is to be humble and grateful. Beautiful Christians with a beautiful heart is a beautiful winning combination!

We are to be men of VALOR and women of EXCELLENCE and it's all in the attitude of gratitude that shows the world the shining star the peacock can truly be as they find that shining bright for Jesus is the #1 fashion accessory and a winning smile is the most important part of your wardrobe!

Meditate on:

1Samuel 16:7b NIV
The LORD does not look at the things people look at. People look at the outward appearance, but the LORD looks at the heart."

FUN FACTS ABOUT PEACOCKS:

A group of Peacocks is called A PARTY!

Peacocks can live up to 40 years!

CINDY BARNES

Chapter 17
THE GOOSE

This is our **ROAD RAGE** Christian! In public they are often very *Loud and Proud* about their faith in Jesus. This Christian many times will be the one with the GIANT "Jesus Loves YOU" Bumper Sticker on their car!

Their Sin is Anger and Lack of Patience ....
They wouldn't like to admit it but they live their lives *'feeling like'* the world owes them something. When talking to the goose you hear throughout their sentences and phrases what sounds like the things they are doing for the Lord is much more important than what others are doing .... getting to their appointment is much more Important than others getting to their appointment.

The following scenario will sound familiar to those who know a goose or to those who are married to a goose, friends with a goose or children of a goose!!

Or is it possible that You, My Friend Are Indeed a Goose?

A Born Again, Set Free and Delivered Goose will sing praises with their loudest voice! They lift their hands in worship and you cannot help but notice their love for the Lord! They "Amen" the Pastors message and "Hallelujah" every exciting point! .... After Church they will be one of the first to go up to shake the Pastors hand and let them know that the message was Powerful and Anointed! As they walk thru the sanctuary and into the lobby you'll hear them commenting to others about the awesome church service...

Then the "UNTHINKABLE" Happens! They get in the car, making sure everyone is buckled up, and begin to back out of the parking slot, then the murmuring begins.... "the idiot in the car behind me could have waited till I'm pulled out" .... Before he/she gets to the driveway he/she begins to feel their blood starting to boil... "UH OH" say the children in the back seat, "not again, please Lord, not again" ...... Soft Prayers come from the mouth of their soulmate in the passenger seat as they hope nobody notices the big ole' "Jesus Loves You" Sticker on the Bumper of their car!

As the GOOSE puts the Pedal to the Metal to take his/her RIGHTFUL PLACE out onto the road the **_Road Rage Begins_** ....

HONK! HONK! HONK! HONK! HONK!

The kids wish they could hide, the soulmate wishes they could disappear, but the goose has already convinced themselves that it's everyone else who should be acting Christ-Like!

A Transformed GOOSE in the Body of Christ shows the world what it looks like to be Big and Bold for Jesus!

It won't be long before those children in the back seat, the soulmate in the passenger seat and all of the people who have ever been on the other side of the gooses wrath will see the transformation too! The goose who has been delivered from self-righteousness, pride, anger and lack of patience will not only become a courteous driver, but courteous in Every Way! .... A BIG Bold Example of Living for Jesus!

Because the heart of every goose is big and bold and they are born with personality plus, they are really one of the most fun types to hang around! It is a wonderful day when you see your friend, the transformed and delivered goose pull out of the parking lot and *yell out the window:*

HONK HONK HONK IF YOU LOVE JESUS!

Meditate on:

Romans 12:2 NIV
Do not conform to the pattern of this world, but be transformed by the renewing of your mind. Then you will be able to test and approve what God's will is - His good, pleasing and perfect will.

FUN FACTS ABOUT GEESE:

Wild geese usually fly in "V" formation because as each goose flaps its wings, it creates an uplift for the other birds behind it and this decreases wind resistance. When the birds in the front get tired other birds from behind replace them. This will extend their flying range 70% compared to when each bird flies alone. Also, the geese behind occasionally honk to encourage those in front to maintain speed.

Geese help and protect other geese that are in trouble. When a goose falls out of the sky due to sickness, wound or when shot, two geese will follow it down. They will stay with it until it dies or is able to fly again. Then they fly out in formation and try to catch the flock.

Such loyalty!

Chapter 18
THE CROW

This is the little Lady of the House! All she ever wanted to be is a great wife and mother, but life and life's situations began to have an effect on her and without knowing it she gave the enemy an inch (he took a mile) – She opened the door of her heart an inch (he got his foot in the door) and eventually and without understanding why, the crow became overwhelmed!

She makes a plan in the morning to greet her hubby at the door in the little Black Slinky Dress he bought her for Christmas. "Yes, that's how I'll greet him" she says! "I'll have the kiddos fed, bathed, prayed for and fast asleep! I'll have a special supper waiting for him with candles burning bright and soft music playing in the background ....

She would even put on a little makeup and her special perfume! …. Yes, this will be a night we will remember for a long time!

As the day goes on the enemy begins messing with her plans. The dog gets up on the counter and pulls the 2 beautiful steaks that she had been marinating onto the kitchen floor! When he realizes he has been caught he swallows an entire steak in one GULP and takes off running with her behind him screaming at the top of her lungs!!!! …. He pauses, Poops on the carpet and flies out the doggie door!

Then her 3 beautiful sweet kiddos arrive home from school! First walks in her *middle child Johnny* who with his head hanging down hands her a note saying he got in trouble today for talking back to the teacher and now she has to schedule a meeting with the principal! …. Next comes her *eldest child Mandy* who informs her that she has been putting off doing a huge project that is ½ of her passing grade into middle school … and YEP, it is due tomorrow!!!! When you tell your daughter that she's going to stay up all night if she has too and get it finished, and NO you are not going to help her with the project, she screams *"I Hate You"* and runs into her bedroom slamming the door behind her! Right as she begins to hyper-ventilate *Sweet Baby Tommy* runs in the front door with the screen door slamming behind him and says, kindergarten was GREAT mom, we had a big party today, and as he turns the corner into the kitchen where she is standing with tears running down her face, thru blurry tear-filled eyes all she sees is a blurry little boy whose face is covered in chocolate, whose hands are a chocolate mess and whose brand new designer shirt that Grandma and Grandpa bought was a RUINED chocolate disaster! Oh My!

That little Black dress did somehow find its way on mom, as she hoped the sweat marks under each arm weren't showing! All 3 kiddos were in their rooms. One doing homework and the other two CRYING! ... The dog was tied up outside and she was sure that the neighbors could hear him howling all the way down the block! ... dinner was, ... well let's just say there wasn't a special candlelight dinner although the matches were lying in the center of the beautiful white table cloth waiting for our little CROW to run to the market to get some candles.... It never did happen that night. (ha)

She gets a text that he is ON HIS WAY and will be home in 10 minutes! His little lady opens her makeup bag and gets the RED Lipstick out that was purchased last week and put aside for what was supposed to be a Perfect Date Night..... She looks in the mirror and thinks to herself that her eyes are now as red as the lipstick....She hears the car pull into the driveway! She panics and puts the lipstick on and runs to the door.... Her plan earlier was to greet him with a glass of sparkling wine and a long kiss after he beholds her beauty and says.... "I AM SUCH A LUCKY MAN!"

She says to herself, *'Help me do this right! Help me make the best of it.'*

The door opens and before he can utter a word, this is what he hears:

SQUAK ... SQUAK ... SQUAK ... SQUAK!

As she bursts into tears and tells him everything that went wrong today and that no matter how hard she tries she just cannot be that woman she "*wants to be*"

The CROW has a tender heart and that is what her hubby fell in love with..... Her heart, not her dress, not her cooking, not their perfect children or her mothering skills ... and after a BIG HUG and Tender Prayers they lit a dollar store bathroom candle, poured sparkling wine into two plastic cups, made a couple of peanut butter and jelly sandwiches and her husband explained to her that a "woman of excellence" isn't excellent because of what she does, but because of who she is! ... then he softly whispered in her ear and she is pretty sure she heard him say:

"I Am Such A Lucky Man"

When you follow "The Recipe" the Cake is Always Good! He reminds her that even when "OUR PLANS" fall thru, it is truly the Lords Plans that will have a lasting effect on what truly matters and that being excellent for Jesus is truly possible every day even when the dog eats the homework or in this case the dinner....

Their night ended well...

Meditate on:

<u>Jeremiah 29:11</u> MSG

I know what I'm doing. I have it all planned out - plans to take care of you, not abandon you, *plans to give you the future you hope for.*

FUN FACTS ABOUT CROWS:

Crows maintain only one mate for their entire life. Once they find their soulmate, it is a lifetime of love and bonding! *(no matter what she makes for dinner or how clean she keeps the nest)*

CINDY BARNES

Chapter 19
THE EAGLE

This is our Isaiah 40:31 Christian! This is our Radical Front-Line Soldier with Wings! This is our goal and hope for *all of us* in the body of Christ! This is close to the heart of every feathered friend we've looked at today thru a *'whimsical birds eye view'*.

All Christ Followers long to soar! Our hearts desire is to keep our eyes upon the Lord! We long to live our lives with determination & purpose, stamina and endurance, balance and especially LOVE!

If every morning we would make it a priority to *'Look Up and watch the SON-rise'* over the Mountains, the Ocean or the Horizon and do our Very Best to remember not only *Who we are but Whose we are ...*

the very poetry and love-song of creation, we will Set ourselves UP for Success as we follow the recipe of God's Holy Word. What an exciting and breathtaking new opportunity and adventure we will experience as we live our lives to the Heart Beat of God. We will truly become the very Melody & Harmony that having intimate fellowship with Father, Son and Holy Spirit will provide us.

Don't Worry, God isn't finished with us yet! We are His workmanship and the very apple of His eye! God never said **"OOPS"** and His plan for us remains intact. Each of us is still learning and growing and no matter who we are or what we've done, it's most important that what we do NEXT lines up with *'The Recipe'* of God's Perfect Plan!

Will we make mistakes? Yep ... Will we ever be perfect? Nope ... but with complete confidence in Jesus who is literally and spiritually transforming us from the inside out, we can boldly hold our head up high, keep our eyes on the Lord, and boldly watch Him transform every obstacle into an opportunity.

Then striving to be the BEST we can be,

As we look in the mirror using God's Recipe,

Filled and fueled with the Spirit surrendered to Thee,

We shall Soar with the Joy that God's Victory Brings,

On the Front Line as Radical Soldiers with Wings!

So what kind of Bird are *'You'* in the body of Christ?

The answer should be *"I'm Fully Surrendered"* and as the King of Kings continues the Good Work within each one of us we will show the world what it *'looks like'* to:

SHINE OUR LIGHT FROM:

THE PERCH WE ARE SITTING ON,

THE GROUND WE ARE TAKING FOR CHRIST,

THE COOP WE ARE MARCHING AROUND,

THE ICEBURG WE ARE SLIDING ON,

THE AIR CURRENT WE ARE CATCHING OR

THE NEST WE ARE BUILDING

And then and only then shall we each realize our full potential as a "Radical Front Line Soldier with Wings.....

As THE OWL
Is no longer known for the gossip of WHO did it or WHO's WHO, but will instead be filled with the Spirit and be known for God's WISDOM and Integrity!

As THE PARROT
No longer REPEATS EVERYTHING they hear UNLESS it is Edifying, Encouraging and Praiseworthy! ... They will be that good example to the OWLS that they always wanted to be and now with the Lord's help will forever be!

As THE OSTRICH
No longer HIDES their head in the sand to run from

their problems, but instead holds their head up high as they RUN TO JESUS casting their cares upon Him and showing the world what it *'Looks Like'* to Live Life **LARGE!**

As THE LARK SPARROW
Begins doing their best to NOT blend in, but takes a stand to Step Out and TEACH OTHERS the *Value & Power of Praise through Prayer & Intercession!*

To be content, filled up and fueled up, ready to respond when the darkness closes in so that the Power of Light will prevail every time!

As THE CANARY
Continues ENCOURAGING OTHERS to be a part of the Worship Team! Leading worship includes musical talent in instruments of praise – in running the sound board – putting up and tearing down the stage for the singers & musicians and being a Top Notch TEAM PLAYER! .... The Canary brings the Melody, the singers bring the Harmony, together with the team they bring the MUSIC which ushers in the BLESSING! ... In Unity it is the Sacrifice of the Highest Praise to God!

As THE PENGUIN
Stops being stuck in Old Traditions where everything they do is BLACK & WHITE but they finally begin to see in Full Color and better yet, Live in Full Color as they *'Choose'* to be led by the Spirit

of the Living God!

And all the Penguins say: "WEEEEEEE"

As THE LOVE BIRDS
Give to GOD the weight of the problems others share with them. They will no longer allow their Gift of Mercy to become the Baggage that Carries the burden that isn't theirs to hold, but instead will become the vehicle that will transport the burdens of others to the Lord in prayer ... This will create Joy in the lifetime journey of loving and serving others!

As THE ROOSTER
No longer comes across as COCKY but will use their amazing voice to teach, reach, edify and encourage! What a wonderful song to hear first thing in the morning! .... Lucky Chickens!

As THE ROADRUNNER
No longer runs from place to place to get a word, a prophecy or a touch from God. But instead they RUN to the Father, who with the Owls Wisdom helps them find a church and a home all in one. A place where they can finally experience being part of a family, where they can get planted, serve, give and grow. Where they can finally know what it is to Be Still in the Presence of the Lord and to finally be "Home Sweet Home".

As THE DOVE
Continues being that strong example of a Spirit-Filled Warrior, living righteously and harming NO ONE!

As THE STORK
Shares with others that "Who You Are" is much more important than "What You Do" and as you do only what the Father asks, you'll never again need to worry that your Many HATS may TOPPLE to the floor or your plate be too full.

As THE TURKEY
No longer GOBBLES UP the time, talent or resources of others, believing they are of no value unless they have a problem that needs fixing, but will begin feeding on God's Word every day and find that their value is in belonging to the Lord. They no longer live in that place of lack and fear but instead thru prayer and *THANKSGIVING* find their place in the family!

As THE VULTURE
Surrenders to the KING and asks the Lord for HIS Daily Fresh Bread. The vulture shall never again settle for 'Day Old Bread' or be defined as being lazy, but instead had simply been misunderstood in the Body of Christ! No longer worried that the vulture will take what is yours, they shall represent one that is well loved by Jesus and well loved by all!

As THE CHICKEN

Chooses to no longer allow FEAR to be the driving force behind what they won't do ... but shall now allow the Lord to be the driving force behind what they will do ... and if they must do it afraid, then by all means *'do it afraid'* and the fear will disappear in the presence of the Living God!

Psalm 34:4

I sought the LORD, and he answered me; he delivered me from all my fear

As THE DUCK

Remembers WHY they Became What They Became and begins to love it again!! A Redcemed Duck Is no longer a QUACK, but shall forever walk in the Breathtaking Beauty of a "Desired Heart"

Psalm 37:4

Take delight in the LORD, and he will give you the desires of your heart.

As THE PEACOCK

No longer goes to church FOR THE LOOKS!

ALL EYES will be on the Peacock who has been transformed into a man or woman of excellence! No longer putting on a show for others to see, but holding high their head as they reflect the Glory of the Lord from within!

As THE GOOSE
Will never again be known as the Road Rage Christian or the HONK HONK in the Body of Christ, but will become that 'vehicle' of Peaceful Courtesy on the Road of Christianity. One that others will strive to be like.

Proverbs 15:1
A **gentle answer turns away wrath**, but harsh words cause quarrels.

So NEXT Time the Redeemed Goose wants to yell out their car window at a crazy driver, they will **stick up their POINTER FINGER** and yell:

GO TO HEAVEN!!!!! ....

As THE CROW
No longer SQUAKS when what she wanted to do is Bless! A dose of friendship with the Dove, the Sparrow and the Canary will help her to become a woman adorned in excellence and covered with God's Peace. As she begins each day with a song of worship & praise the Spirit of God shall permeate the room and open the door for God's Presence to touch every corner of her mind will and emotions helping her to be that true and loving blessing, and woman, wife & mother she can be proud of as she radiates His Divine EXCELLENCE.

IN CLOSING

We are all a part of a BIGGER Family and as we stick together, learn from our mistakes and the mistakes of others, encourage one another to continue learning & growing, *KEEP Shining*, *KEEP Doing* the hard right things that make Jesus proud, and with the strength of Christ make a promise to endure till the end, you will be able to say, as I will be able to say, and everyone reading this book will be able to say... as **Radical Christian Soldiers with Wings** .....

DON'T LET THE FEATHERS FOOL YA! ...
hope you enjoyed the journey!